Investing in Cryptocurrency

A Beginner's Guide to Mastering the Digital Economy

Table of Contents

Chapter 1. Introduction

Understanding the intricacies of the modern financial landscape may seem daunting, especially when it comes to the digital economy. This is where our Special Report on "Investing in Cryptocurrency: A Beginner's Guide to Mastering the Digital Economy" comes into play. Steering away from overly technical jargon, this report is crafted with the beginner in mind, presenting topics in an easily understandable, digestible form. We approach this revolutionary financial frontier with pragmatism, breaking down complex principles into straightforward language. The goal? To equip you with the knowledge you need to confidently navigate cryptocurrency investing and make informed decisions in this dynamic digital arena. Remember, understanding is the first step on the journey to mastery. This report is more than a guide; it's your trustworthy companion as you step into the exciting world of cryptocurrency investing.

Chapter 2. Understanding Cryptocurrency: A Brief History

The unique birth and development of cryptocurrencies begin with the introduction of Bitcoin, the first ever cryptocurrency, in 2009. Bitcoin, created by an individual or group of individuals using the pseudonym Satoshi Nakamoto, was conceived as an alternative to government-controlled currencies. Satoshi's white paper, titled 'Bitcoin: A Peer-to-Peer Electronic Cash System,' introduced the idea of a decentralized peer-to-peer payment system.

2.1. The Birth of Bitcoin

No account of the history of cryptocurrency can begin without mentioning the 2008 economic crisis. This period saw widespread disillusionment with traditional banking systems and governments due to large-scale financial instability. It was during this period, particularly the fall of 2008, that the domain name bitcoin.org was registered. Shortly thereafter, the aforementioned white paper was published on this site.

This revolutionary Bitcoin white paper suggested that money could be sent directly from one party to another without going through third-party intermediaries such as banks. Nakamoto called this a peer-to-peer network, and he devised a way for these transactions to be publicly recorded on what he referred to as a blockchain.

2.2. Understanding Blockchain

The blockchain provided the foundation of Bitcoin and, later, other cryptocurrencies. This technology allowed these peer-to-peer transactions to be tracked and recorded in a public ledger. The blockchain solved the key problem inherent in digital currencies, which is the risk of double-spending – the same single digital coin being spent more than once. This is achieved through a process known as mining, whereby powerful computers perform complicated calculations to validate and record transactions on the blockchain. Moreover, it also ensured that there could be no interference by government agencies or banks.

2.3. The Diversification of Cryptocurrencies

In the years following the creation of Bitcoin, many new cryptocurrencies (often termed altcoins) began to appear. Each sought to improve on or completely change some aspect of Bitcoin's design. Some became successful, while others fell by the wayside.

In 2011, a software developer named Charlie Lee created Litecoin, a peer-to-peer cryptocurrency that offered faster transaction confirmation times than Bitcoin. Its efficient algorithm allowed miners to produce 84 million Litecoins, significantly more than the 21 million total Bitcoin limit.

Around the same time, Namecoin was developed, aiming to use the same peer-to-peer network as Bitcoin to make internet censorship more difficult. An individual could record a site on Namecoin's blockchain, making it virtually impossible to block.

Perhaps most notably, in 2015, Ethereum was launched. Ethereum took the blockchain technology of Bitcoin and expanded its capabilities significantly. Rather than just being a platform for sending and receiving digital money, Ethereum allowed developers to create a wide range of applications that functioned directly on its blockchain. The Ethereum network also popularized the use of smart contracts, self-executing contracts with the terms of the agreement directly written into code.

2.4. The Age of ICOs

The mid-2010s also saw the rise of Initial Coin Offerings (ICOs), a type of crowdfunding using cryptocurrencies. An ICO is when a crypto startup sells a predetermined number of digital tokens to the public to fund the development of a product or service.

ICOs gained significant traction in 2017, raising billions of dollars for numerous projects. However, many of these have ended in disaster, with projects failing to deliver on their promises or turning out to be outright scams. This led to a broader skepticism around ICOs, resulting in stricter oversight by financial regulators and a drop in popularity of this method.

2.5. Cryptocurrencies Today

Today, there are over 7,000 cryptocurrencies traded in different platforms, each promising its unique features and uses. Bitcoin continues to hold the highest market cap among all, having become both a popular digital asset and a societal phenomenon. Cryptocurrencies have moved out of the fringes of the tech world and are now considered a legitimate part of the financial industry. Their decentralised nature and resistance to censorship make them attractive for transactions. At the same time, they continue to be the subject of intense debate and scrutiny.

To conclude, the history of cryptocurrencies is a testament to our collective desire for greater financial autonomy and alternatives to traditional monetary systems. It also unequivocally hints at how this digital landscape will continue to evolve with new technologies and market dynamics once unimaginable. The road to mastery of this digital frontier, like history, would likely remain full of ups and downs, unexpected turns, and unprecedented opportunities.

Chapter 3. The Essence of Blockchain: Decentralization and Security

Blockchain technology, the innovative digital architecture underpinning cryptocurrencies, combines notions of decentralization and security to create a network that dramatically shifts traditional constructs of trust and authority. While efforts to comprehend the parameters of this technology may appear challenging, it largely revolves around these two fundamental principles.

3.1. Decentralization: Shifting Control and Transparency

Let's begin by looking at decentralization, a concept markedly distinct from the centralization that traditionally characterizes finance. Decentralized systems divide control equitably among all users, resulting in networks where no one individual or group exercises dominant influence. This is a profound departure from classic centralized systems, where a small group or a single institution, such as a bank or government, retains control over assets and operations.

In a decentralized blockchain network, a publicly viewable ledger records every transaction. This means any network participant can verify transaction history, ensuring unprecedented transparency. This is contrary to centralized models where a single trusted intermediary validates transactions. The shift from trust in institutions to trust in the protocol is revolutionizing the financial landscape—perspectives and behaviors are rewritten with the transparency and democratic ethos integral to blockchain-based platforms.

3.2. Security: Trust, Transaction Verification, and Immutability

Security, another cornerstone of the blockchain concept, intertwines with decentralization. Trustworthiness in a blockchain network doesn't hinge on an individual party's integrity, but on the infallibility of the network's protocols. Such security is mainly achieved through two mechanisms: transaction verification and immutability.

Transaction verification falls to "miners" in blockchain networks, executing a process known as proof-of-work. They solve complex calculations, verifying transactions and adding them to the blockchain. This procedure guards against double-spending (an instance where an individual spends a cryptocurrency unit more than once) and ensures the integrity of the transaction history.

Moreover, the blockchain's design makes it immutable. Immutability means that once a block is added to the chain, changing or removing it becomes practically impossible. Malicious actors would need overwhelming computational power to alter past transactions—considerably more than half of the entire network's processing capability—a scenario highly improbable due to the decentralized nature of blockchain networks.

3.3. Disruptive Potential

The robust blend of decentralization and security in the blockchain design has dramatic implications for various sectors. It reduces reliance on central intermediaries—initiating a shift from trust-based systems to ones rooted in cryptographic proof. This shift decreases costs linked to validation, record-keeping, and fraudulent transactions while influencing existing power relations, dynamic economies, and social structures.

3.4. Participating in the Blockchain

To partake in blockchain transactions, a user requires a public and a private key—an identity token in the decentralized ledger. The public key is a user's address, while the private key securely authorizes transactions.

Blockchain networks approve transactions through consensus mechanisms. Approval requires agreement from the majority of nodes—devices running the blockchain software. This verification system ensures that only valid transactions make their way into the blockchain, furthering the overall network security.

3.5. Decentralization and Security: A New Frontier

In sum, the profound merger of decentralization and security forms the heart of blockchain technology—a disruptive phenomenon bound to reshape the foundations of multiple sectors. The transparency, flexibility, and trust endowed by this model present countless opportunities, sparking a new era in the global economy. As this digital frontier continues to evolve and mature, understanding blockchain's core principles will be fundamental to navigating cryptocurrency markets and beyond.

Blockchain's intricacies might seem daunting at first, but at its core, it's an elegant fusion of classic concepts. The fundamental elements of decentralization and security, brought together in this novel way, offer a new perspective on how resources can be managed, transferred, and stored—and understanding these principles is the key to unlocking blockchain's full potential. Now armed with this understanding, you're well-equipped to explore the broader realm of cryptocurrency investing with informed confidence.

Chapter 4. Types of Cryptocurrencies: More Than Just Bitcoin

The age of digital currencies has arrived, and while Bitcoin might have been the first, it is certainly not the last. We now exist in a world where there are over 4,000 cryptocurrencies that investors can potentially buy. Let's dig into this expansive landscape to clarify what constitutes a "cryptocurrency," explore some of the different types available, and equip you with the knowledge needed to make informed decisions.

4.1. Understanding Cryptocurrencies

To start, we need to understand what a cryptocurrency is. In simple terms, a cryptocurrency is a digital or virtual form of currency that uses cryptography for security. This makes it extremely difficult to counterfeit or double-spend. Most cryptocurrencies are based on a technology called blockchain – a distributed ledger enforced by a disparate network of computers.

One important thing to note about cryptocurrencies is that they are decentralized. Unlike traditional 'fiat' currencies like the US Dollar or Euro which are controlled by central banks, cryptocurrencies are not controlled by any central authority. This can make them immune to government interference or manipulation.

4.2. Bitcoin: The Genesis of Cryptocurrencies

Bitcoin was the first-ever cryptocurrency, and it remains by far the most well-known and valuable. Invented in 2008 by an unidentified person (or group of people) using the name Satoshi Nakamoto, Bitcoin introduced us to the revolutionary blockchain technology.

Bitcoin is traded via a decentralized ledger system known as the blockchain. The Bitcoin protocol – the rules that make Bitcoin work – say that only 21 million Bitcoins can ever be created by miners.

This limitation is a significant factor in Bitcoin's value; it also makes Bitcoin a potential hedge against inflation, similar to gold. As the world discovers an increasing number of applications for cryptocurrencies, Bitcoin remains the primary measuring stick by which all others are judged.

4.3. Altcoins: The Bitcoin Alternatives

While it's natural to focus on Bitcoin, it isn't the entire story. Thousands of alternative coins ("altcoins") have sprung up, many of which offer compelling use cases and innovative approaches. Some altcoins are spin-offs of Bitcoin, known as 'forks,' created by altering Bitcoin's original code, with variations in coin processing speeds, security protocol, or consensus mechanisms. Litecoin, for example, is a Bitcoin spin-off with a faster processing speed proposed as a solution for small transactions.

Other altcoins emerge with completely novel infrastructure and purpose. For instance, Ethereum – an altcoin that extends beyond the financial use case – created the potential for "smart contracts" using blockchain technology. To put it simply, smart contracts are programs that execute exactly as they are set up to by their creators. Ethereum's native cryptocurrency is Ether, which powers these smart contracts within the network.

Ripple, on the other hand, is a real-time global settlement network that aims to enable fast, low-cost international money transfers. Ripple's digital token, XRP, plays a crucial role in this process, acting as a bridge between different fiat currencies.

4.4. Tokenization: The Future of Investment?

A new trend in the world of cryptocurrencies is the rise of tokens representing a particular fungible and tradable asset, or a utility that's often found on a blockchain. Tokens are versatile in their application; they can represent anything from a store of value, a set of services to access, or even an underlying asset (real estate, stocks, etc.).

Unlike coins that have their own separate blockchains, tokens are built and distributed on existing blockchain networks. The Ethereum network, which allows for easier token creation, is a popular choice for token issuance.

Security tokens represent an actual interest in a company, much like a share in traditional investing. They've been called the intersection of digital assets and traditional financial products. On the other hand, utility tokens grant the holder access to a network's features and services.

4.5. Privacy Coins: The Future of Anonymity?

While Bitcoin and most cryptocurrencies offer some level of privacy, it's not absolute. Privacy coins are a special category specifically designed to maintain the privacy and anonymity of the transaction participants. Zcash, for example, allows users to make transactions without revealing the amount, recipient, or sender, using highly advanced cryptographic techniques. Monero, another privacy-focused coin, is highly favored due to its dynamic scalability and mandatory privacy features, making all transactions on the network anonymous by default.

Exploring the world of cryptocurrencies is akin to navigating uncharted waters. There's an element of unpredictability tied with fluctuating prices, regulatory changes, technological advancements, and so forth. But with an understanding of the various types of cryptocurrencies, you're better equipped to decide which digital coins and tokens may be worth considering for investment.

It's clear that while cryptocurrencies are an exciting development in the world of finance, it's essential to perform your own due diligence before deciding in which you should invest. The universe of cryptocurrencies has a lot to offer, and this primer should serve as a springboard as you dive deeper to explore each asset's potential. Happy investing!

Chapter 5. Wallets and Exchanges: Safeguarding Your Digital Assets

As an integral part of your crypto journey, you'll encounter wallets and exchanges. These two tools are essential in managing and safeguarding your digital assets. This chapter delves into these topics, equipping you with the skills needed to use these tools proficiently and safely.

In the realms of cryptocurrency, wallets and exchanges serve as your bank and stock exchange respectively. To grasp their roles fully, we'll cover each tool starting with wallets, then proceeding to exchanges, and wrapping up with useful tips to safeguard your digital assets.

5.1. Understanding Cryptocurrency Wallets

A crypto wallet is a tool that allows you to store and manage your digital coins. In reality, it doesn't technically hold your crypto. Instead, it stores pairs of public and private keys - cryptographic codes that establish your ownership of the coins and enable transactions.

Crypto wallets can be broadly divided into five types, each with its pros and cons:

1. Hot Wallets: These are internet-connected wallets, and while they're convenient, they are more susceptible to online threats.

2. Cold Wallets: Opposite to hot wallets, these are not connected to the internet and therefore offer a higher level of security.

3. Desktop Wallets: These are software packages you can download and install on your PC or laptop.

4. Mobile Wallets: These are apps designed for smartphones, providing convenience and mobility.

5. Hardware Wallets: These are physical devices that store your keys offline, providing an extra layer of security.

The choice of wallet depends on your specific needs and risk tolerance. A prudent practice is to keep a major portion of your holdings in more secure wallets like cold or hardware wallets, and a smaller fraction in easily accessible hot wallets.

5.2. Navigating through Cryptocurrency Exchanges

Once you figure out where to store your cryptocurrency, the next step is to learn how to acquire it. This generally happens on crypto exchanges, online platforms where traders buy and sell digital coins using traditional money or other digital currencies.

Exchanges are not all the same - they vary in terms of security features, user interfaces, supported cryptocurrencies, fees, and more. Some common types include:

1. Centralized Exchanges (CEXs) - These are run by third-party providers who control the platform. They are user-friendly but more vulnerable to hacks.

2. Decentralized Exchanges (DEXs) - They allow peer-to-peer trading without intermediaries, offering more privacy but are less intuitive.

3. Hybrid Exchanges - These platforms seek to combine the best features of the two types mentioned above.

Avoid jumping into the first exchange you come across. Do your homework - evaluate different platforms, check their reputation, and identify one that provides the right balance between ease of use and security.

5.3. Safeguarding Your Digital Assets

The digital nature of cryptocurrencies makes them vulnerable to several risks. Adopting robust safety measures is key to securing your assets:

1. Multi-factor authentication: Enable this feature. It requires you to validate your identity by providing at least two authentication factors before accessing the account.

2. Cold or Offline Storage: Keeping assets in an offline environment prevents unauthorized access.

3. Secure Internet Connection: Always execute your transactions over a secure connection, preferably a trusted private network.

Keeping track of your transaction details: Make a habit of recording details such as wallet addresses, transaction IDs, dates, and amounts. This will be handy in case of disagreements or disputes.

Despite all the precautions, if you find yourself in a security breach always report it immediately to the relevant people and take necessary steps to minimize loss such as changing passwords or transferring your assets to another safe wallet.

Remember that the architecture of blockchain and cryptocurrencies is designed to be secure, but the devices you use to access them might not be. Hence, the more you know and implement safety measures, the less likely you will be to fall victim to digital theft - knowledge truly is your best defense.

While wallets and exchanges could seem complicated at first, they become less daunting once you understand their workings. Keep abreast of latest developments and safety practices and ensure you always protect your digital assets like you would your real-life valuables. Remember, effective management and safeguarding of digital assets is crucial for successful crypto investing. Don't rush, take your time, and learn the ropes properly. There are no shortcuts to success in the crypto world.

That's it for wallets and exchanges! In the following chapter, we'll delve deeper into the world of blockchain, the technology that underpins cryptocurrency. Understanding this is an essential part of the crypto-journey, so don't miss it!

Chapter 6. Investment Strategies: Navigating the Cryptocurrency Market

Cryptocurrency, as an asset class, is unique. It is characterized by extreme volatility, speculation, and a substantial potential for return. Unlike traditional investment strategies where historical data, economic forces, and market sentiment form a densely-woven tapestry of insight, the relatively nascent nature of cryptocurrency presents investors with a landscape that's yet to be thoroughly mapped.

Seeking the correct investment strategies in such a terrain can seem formidable. However, this chapter aims to demystify the process, bringing to bear a pragmatic approach to cryptocurrency investment intended to empower investors to make informed decisions in this arena.

6.1. Understanding the Market Dynamics

Before diving into investment strategies, it's crucial to understand the unique dynamics that shape the cryptocurrency market. In particular, two key factors:

1. Volatility: Cryptocurrencies are infamous for their dramatic price swings. Bitcoin, for instance, saw its value rocket to nearly $20,000 in late 2017, only to plummet to around $3,000 the following year—a stark illustration of the market's inherent volatility. This makes timing one's investment more challenging, yet also opens the door to significant profit potential.

2. Decentralization: Unlike   traditional   asset   classes,

cryptocurrencies are decentralized. This means they're not regulated by any central authority like a government or a central bank. They operate on blockchain technology, which ensures transparency and security of transactions but also leaves the field open for wild price swings.

These factors contribute to cryptocurrency's high-risk, high-reward nature, which might not be suitable for conservative investors but could be attractive for those willing to accept higher levels of risk for greater potential returns.

6.2. Fundamental Analysis

While cryptocurrencies operate under a different rule set than traditional economies, the process of evaluating them holds parallels to classical investment analysis. Much like traditional investments, understanding the fundamentals of a crypto asset can help in determining its potential value.

When we talk about fundamentals in cryptocurrency, we are generally talking about its real-world utility, the soundness of its underlying technology, the strength and commitment of its development team, market sentiment, and other technical signals. These indicators provide insights into potential price movements over time.

6.3. Technical Analysis

While fundamental analysis evaluates intrinsic value, technical analysis is entirely fixated on statistics generated by market activity, such as past prices and volume.

Patterns within these movements are analyzed to identify trends, which traders can then extrapolate to predict future price movements. A wide range of techniques are employed in this conversion, from simple moving averages to complex machine learning algorithms.

When used in conjunction with fundamental analysis, technical analysis can give investors both a macro-level view of the market (from fundamental analysis) and a micro-level understanding of specific trading opportunities (through technical analysis).

6.4. Diversification and Risk Management

Given the nature of the cryptocurrency market, risk management is essential. Even the most seasoned investors cannot avoid risk entirely, but they can take steps to mitigate it. One widely adopted practice is portfolio diversification. This means spreading investments across a variety of cryptocurrencies.

In the crypto context, an investor might split their holdings across a variety of coins, such as Bitcoin, Ethereum, and a selection of alternative coins (Altcoins). Given the correlation between different cryptocurrency prices, a diversified portfolio generally carves a smaller risk profile than a portfolio focusing on a single coin.

6.5. Dollar-Cost Averaging

Dollar-cost averaging (DCA) is a strategy where an investor divides their total investment amount into periodic purchases of a target asset to reduce the impact of volatility.

Consider an investor who wants to invest $1,000 in Bitcoin. Instead of buying $1,000 worth of Bitcoin on a single day, under DCA, they might purchase $100 worth of Bitcoin every Monday for 10 weeks. This can fortify the investor against short-term price swings.

6.6. Active Trading vs. Hold Strategy

Active trading involves buying and selling cryptocurrencies over short periods to profit from market fluctuations. Day trading and swing trading are two common forms of active trading. However, these require a significant time investment, a deep understanding of the market, and a high risk tolerance.

Alternatively, a 'Hold' Strategy (from 'Hold On for Dear Life') involves buying and holding a cryptocurrency long-term, banking on appreciation over time. This can be a low-stress approach for those who believe in the technology's long-term prospects.

6.7. Beware of Common Pitfalls

Mistakes are part of the investment journey. But awareness of common pitfalls—like emotionally-driven decision making, lackluster research, or failure to understand a coin's underlying technology—can make the difference between a profitable investment and a costly mistake.

To avoid these traps, establish a disciplined investment regimen. Develop structured research techniques, employ disciplined money management, and always allocate an amount you can afford to lose.

6.8. Staying Informed

As the market evolves, staying informed about new developments is essential. Regularly engage with news outlets, industry experts, and dedicated crypto communities. Continuous learning is a cornerstone of successful investing, especially in an area as fluid as cryptocurrency.

Investing in cryptocurrencies could be the investment opportunity of a lifetime. But like any investment, it requires an analytical approach, a well-crafted investment strategy, and a significant amount of research. Remember, never invest money you cannot afford to lose, and always do your due diligence before making any investment decisions.

Chapter 7. Risk Management: Safeguarding Your Investment Portfolio Against Volatility

Maintaining a balanced portfolio is paramount in managing the marked volatility inherent in the crypto-market. This is achieved mainly by thoughtful asset allocation, regular rebalancing, understanding and applying risk tolerance, and by having a solid exit strategy in place. All these concepts will be discussed in detail throughout this chapter to help provide a well-rounded insight into effective risk management strategies in cryptocurrency investment.

7.1. Understanding and Applying Risk Tolerance

Knowledge is the key to gaining mastery in any field, and understanding your risk tolerance is certainly no exception when it comes to managing your cryptocurrency investments. Risk tolerance fundamentally refers to your ability and willingness to endure losses, which is crucial given the potential for severe market volatility in the digital economy.

To determine your risk tolerance, you must first conduct an honest appraisal of your financial situation and goals. Are you in a position where you can handle a sudden significant loss in your portfolio's value, or could such a downturn drastically affect your living standards? If you're planning longer-term investments aimed at a future goal, your tolerance for short-term volatility could increase.

In this digital realm, investors are often swayed by the tale of astronomical gains, leading to higher risk-taking. However, it's imperative to remember that high returns often come with high risks. A sound understanding of your personal level of risk tolerance is crucial to ensure that you make informed and sensible choices.

7.2. Diversifying Your Portfolio

After acknowledging your risk tolerance, the next strategy is portfolio diversification. The age-old adage, "Don't put all your eggs in one basket," best describes this approach. Cryptocurrency offers a wealth of different asset choices, ranging from the more established tokens like Bitcoin (BTC) and Ethereum (ETH) to a wealth of altcoins.

However, the trick to successful diversification is not to simply own several different currencies, but to invest within diverse sectors in the crypto universe. For instance, you might split your investments across decentralized finance (DeFi) tokens, utility tokens, and perhaps a smattering of non-fungible tokens (NFTs).

Some investors also choose to diversify across different blockchains to spread their potential risk. For instance, someone might opt for a mixture of Ethereum-based coins, Binance Smart Chain tokens, and maybe a few from the Solana ecosystem.

There's no one-size-fits-all approach, and it's crucial to do thorough research on the potential and stability of different currencies and sectors before investing.

7.3. Regular Rebalancing

As prices fluctuate, so too will the composition of your portfolio. If a particular asset performs well, it might start to take up a larger portion of your portfolio, which could increase your exposure to risk if the price of that asset abruptly falls. This is where the concept of rebalancing comes into play.

Regular rebalancing of your portfolio involves adjusting your holdings to maintain the desired allocation ratio. There are two main strategies: the calendar method (rebalancing at set intervals, e.g., quarterly or annually) and the threshold method (rebalancing when a particular asset type exceeds a certain portion of your portfolio). There are pros and cons to both methods, with the calendar method being more predictable and the threshold method being more responsive to market conditions.

Yet, it's important to note that rebalancing often implies the selling of assets that are performing well and buying those that are not. Although this might seem counterintuitive, successful rebalancing requires adhering to predetermined strategies rather than succumbing to emotional trading impulses.

7.4. Setting a Solid Exit Strategy

Finally, and perhaps most crucially, effective risk management involves setting a well-considered exit strategy. Essentially, this means deciding under which conditions you would sell or convert your assets. It could be that you've reached a predetermined target price, or that a particular investment is consistently underperforming.

Having a comprehensive exit strategy helps negate emotional or panicked decisions in reaction to market trends. Write it down, stick to it, and avoid the temptation of "just one more day" if the conditions for exit have been met. Keep in mind that in the erratic world of cryptocurrency, sometimes the best win is to minimize losses.

In conclusion, managing risk within the volatile environment of cryptocurrency investment necessarily requires thoughtful consideration and the disciplined application of a range of strategies. Due consideration to your level of risk tolerance, diversification of your portfolio, regular rebalancing, and the establishment of a robust exit strategy will all contribute to the safeguarding of your investments. Remember, informed decision-making is your most powerful tool in navigating the digital economic landscape.

Chapter 8. Analysing Crypto Trend: Forecasting Market Changes

Every experienced investor knows that understanding trends is key to forecasting market changes, and this is no different in the world of cryptocurrencies. But with the sheer volume of information and minute-by-minute fluctuation of prices, how do you sift through the noise and make sense of the trends?

8.1. Considering Market Basics

To begin with, understanding financial markets and their mechanics is crucial. The first thing to remember is that cryptocurrencies, much like traditional assets, are driven by supply and demand dynamics. In the broadest sense, if a crypto asset's demand surpasses its supply, its price will rise. Conversely, if the supply exceeds demand, the price will fall. It might sound simple, but pinning down these dynamics within a market as volatile and unpredictable as cryptocurrency can be tricky.

8.2. Understanding Cryptocurrency Volatility

Crypto market volatility refers to the rapid and significant price movements that can happen within short periods of time – moving upwards or downwards. In traditional financial markets, volatility is often seen as a risk. However, in the context of the crypto market, volatility can also provide unique investment and trading opportunities.

Identifying the causes of such volatility is key. Several factors stimulate these movements, including technological updates, media coverage, market sentiment, regulatory news, and macroeconomic trends, among others. Moreover, the psychology of investors—driven by fear and greed—also plays a significant role. By understanding what drives this volatility, you can anticipate potential pivots in the market trend.

8.3. The Role of Technical Analysis

Technical analysis represents an essential tool for crypto trend analysis. It relies on the study of statistical trends gathered from trading activity, such as price movement and volume. This form of analysis does not consider a cryptocurrency's intrinsic value but instead uses historical trading data to determine potential price direction.

There are various technical analysis tools available, but three of the most common ones include moving averages, Relative Strength Index (RSI), and Fibonacci Retracement.

1. **Moving Averages** are used to identify the direction of a trend and smooth out price fluctuations to create a clear line that represents the average price over a distinct period. The two most common types are the Simple Moving Average (SMA) and the Exponential Moving Average (EMA). The latter places more weight on recent price data and reacts more quickly to price changes.

2. **Relative Strength Index (RSI)** is used to identify oversold or overbought conditions in a market. When the RSI crosses above a certain threshold (typically 70), the asset is considered overbought, and a market correction might be on the horizon. Conversely, if it crosses below another threshold (usually 30), the asset is thought to be oversold and might experience upward pressure.

3. **Fibonacci Retracement** is a tool that draws horizontal lines to indicate areas of support or resistance at the key Fibonacci levels before the price continues in the original direction. These levels are 23.6%, 38.2%, 50%, 61.8%, and 100%. Traders use these levels as a guide to gauge potential price reactions.

8.4. Fundamental Analysis in the Crypto Space

While technical analysis focuses on the "when" to buy, fundamental analysis shines a light on the "what" to buy. It involves an evaluation of the intrinsic value of a cryptocurrency by considering various indicators such as the coin's market capitalization, the circulating supply, the total supply, and the coin's use cases.

Significant focus should be placed on a coin's use case, as this often determines a cryptocurrency's long-term value and sustainability. Cryptocurrencies with strong use cases and robust technology are more likely to withstand market volatility and deliver long-term return on investment.

8.5. Utilizing Crypto News and Market Sentiment

As mentioned earlier, fear and greed often drive the crypto markets. Therefore, keeping a pulse on market sentiment is especially important. This sentiment can often be gauged through news and social media platforms. News about a government regulation or a major hack on a digital wallet company can precipitate significant price swings.

Moreover, the introduction of sentiment analysis tools, which use AI to interpret market sentiment from social media and news headlines, are becoming an increasingly important part of a crypto investor's toolbox.

8.6. Evaluating Historical Price Trends

Reviewing cryptocurrencies' historical price trends can provide valuable insights for current and future investments. Looking at long-term trends can help distinguish between short-term volatility and a more permanent change.

While historical performance is by no means a guarantee of future results, these historical patterns can help forecast future trends, especially when used in combination with other analytical tools.

8.7. Conclusion

Analysing crypto trends and forecasting market changes involve a wide array of techniques and require an understanding of both fundamental factors and technical analytics. By equipping yourself with these vital tools and constantly staying informed about the evolving landscape, you will be well-prepared for your investment journey. Remember, investing is not about predicting the future but about making informed decisions and managing risk effectively.

Chapter 9. Regulatory Environment and Legal Considerations: Navigating the Legal Maze

Indulging in cryptocurrency trading or investing is an emerging area which is still largely unregulated in most parts of the world. While on the one hand, some countries have wholeheartedly embraced the potential of blockchain technology and cryptocurrencies, other countries have given a more skeptical or cautious response, leading to a complex legal environment which requires careful navigation. Being aware of these legal norms is critical to avoid any legal pitfalls or penalties that come with non-compliance.

9.1. Blockchain Technology: A Paradigm Shift in Economy

The concept of blockchain technology was first introduced through the invention of Bitcoin, the first virtual currency, by an individual or group under the pseudonym Satoshi Nakamoto. The technology is essentially a decentralized system storing transactional records, where the users are in control, as opposed to existing centralized systems where a single entity, like a bank, has full control.

Even though it was invented as a transactional platform, blockchain has evolved to serve multiple purposes – from creating other cryptocurrencies to digital contracts, identity management, and data storage. The adoption of this decentralized, distributed ledger technology has transformed industries across the globe, offering new ways of engaging in traditional practices. This has incurred significant legal and regulatory attention, focusing on aspects like privacy, security, contract law, and business transactions.

9.2. Global Stance on Cryptocurrencies

Different countries have taken different stances on cryptocurrencies - from outright banning to wholehearted acceptance.

Let's consider the case of a few countries:

1. China has taken an extremely harsh line against cryptocurrencies, banning their use and trade actively.

2. United States, being a federal system, doesn't have a uniform policy across all its states. The Securities and Exchange Commission has been largely positive, warning investors about possible risks but also allowing for registered crypto exchanges.

3. Countries like Japan and Switzerland have been highly supportive of cryptocurrencies, passing laws that recognize digital currencies as legal tender and encouraging crypto businesses.

Knowing the stance of your nation on crypto can go a long way in ensuring that your engagement with cryptocurrencies doesn't fall into any legal grey areas.

9.3. Regulatory Environment: Therapeutic Uncertainty

One of the key characteristics of cryptocurrencies is their volatility, largely because they operate in a regulatory grey area. Laws and regulations are often reactive and find it difficult to keep up with the blitzkrieg pace of technological advancement. Additionally, regulatory bodies by their very nature tend to be conservative, and the disruptive potential of cryptocurrencies doesn't appeal much to them.

In many jurisdictions, laws are yet to be written to even classify whether cryptocurrencies come under currencies, commodities, or securities. This poses a significant challenge for cryptocurrency holders and investors. For instance, if Bitcoin is considered a currency, investors may have to pay capital gains tax on it.

9.4. Legal Considerations for Crypto Investors

In the face of all these uncertainties, there are some precautions that one can take to avoid legal trouble:

1. Always pay taxes on gains: The regulatory ambiguity surrounding cryptocurrencies does not exempt them from tax obligations. Any profit made from the sale of cryptocurrencies should typically be declared as capitals gains to your respective tax authority.

2. Know the KYC and AML requirements: Most crypto exchanges require stringent Know Your Customer (KYC) and Anti-Money Laundering (AML) checks. Ensure you comply with these norms and keep detailed records of your transactions.

3. Comply with securities laws: If your cryptocurrency activities involve issuing or trading assets that could be classified as securities, be sure to comply with relevant securities laws. Remember, just because a cryptocurrency isn't currently classified as a security doesn't mean it won't be in the future.

4. Legal advice is crucial: Depend on legal advice for understanding the implications of regulatory frameworks on your crypto investments, especially when it comes to matters of tax liability and compliance with laws.

Cryptocurrency has entered and influenced every legal area from contract law to consumer protection, tax law and more, making it essential for investors to understand these interconnections. But this complexity and navigating the maze should not discourage you. The more you understand, the better equipped you are to stay compliant and faceless risk, ultimately making wiser investment decisions.

9.5. Cryptocurrency v/s Traditional Economy: A Complex Relationship

The convenience of digital cash and investment avenues creates a significant overlap between cryptocurrencies and traditional banking. Banks and financial institutions have remained wary of cryptocurrencies, perceived as a challenge to their traditional role. They are wrestling with cryptocurrencies' potential impact on their operations, financial stability, and monetary policy.

On the one hand, cryptocurrencies could replace the existing banking infrastructure if they gain mass adoption. On the other hand, using blockchain technology and decentralized finance mechanisms, banks could innovate their services, offering secure, cheap, and fast transactions.

Even though the legal landscape for cryptocurrencies is hazy and ever-evolving, having a basic understanding of the rules and regulations that impact crypto investments is key to a successful cryptocurrency investment journey. But remember, laws are constantly changing, and keeping abreast with this dynamic legal landscape will require constant learning and adaptation.

While cryptocurrencies can be disruptive, they represent a unique and potentially lucrative investment opportunity. With due diligence, awareness, and legal guidance, even beginners can climb the steep learning curve and start making informed decisions in the world of cryptocurrency trading and investment.

In the face of these realities, regulation will be crucial to protect consumers and maintain financial stability, while not stifling the potential of digital currencies. Through this continuous journey of learning, layer by layer, you will understand that a complex regulatory environment is not a barrier but a guide, navigating you through the legal maze towards mastering the digital economy.

Chapter 10. Tax Implications of Cryptocurrency Investments

Cryptocurrency has rapidly evolved from being a technological marvel to a popular investment vehicle. As an investor, it's vital to understand the tax implications related to your cryptocurrency investments. This knowledge will not only enhance your investing skills but will also allow you to maximize your returns legally and efficiently.

10.1. Setting the Groundwork: Basics of Cryptocurrency Taxes

Let's begin by taking a look at the essential facet of cryptocurrency investments - cryptocurrency is treated as a property for tax purposes. This means that, like real estate or stocks, it is subject to capital gains tax. When you buy and sell cryptocurrency, tax obligations are triggered.

The key component here is the capital gain or loss. The taxable event occurs when a capital gain is realized, which essentially means that you've sold the cryptocurrency for more than you've spent acquiring it. This principle applies even if you exchange one cryptocurrency for another. For instance, if you bought Bitcoin for $500 and sold it for $800, your capital gain would be $300.

Identifying the tax is relatively straightforward: if you held the cryptocurrency for less than a year, it's considered short-term capital gain, and the regular income tax rates would apply. In contrast, if you held it for more than a year, it would fall under long-term capital gains, presenting potentially lower rates.

10.2. Taxable Events in Cryptocurrency

Several events within the realm of cryptocurrency investing trigger tax obligations. They range from selling your cryptocurrency for fiat currency, exchanging one cryptocurrency for another, and even using cryptocurrency to purchase goods or services.

But not all transactional activities are taxable. Buying and holding cryptocurrency does not bring tax obligations unless you've sold or exchanged it. Similarly, transferring your cryptocurrencies between your wallets isn't a taxable event, despite being technically a send/receive mechanism.

10.3. Calculating Capital Gains from Cryptocurrency

To calculate the capital gains from your cryptocurrency investments, you would first need to establish your cost basis, which includes the amount you spent to acquire the cryptocurrency, including fees, commissions, and other acquisition costs.

Subtracting the cost basis from your sale proceeds will give you your capital gain or loss. If you've sold multiple positions throughout the year, you'll have to calculate the gain or loss individually and then aggregate them for your taxable income.

10.4. Record Keeping for Cryptocurrency Investments

Maintaining accurate records is an indispensable part of managing the tax implications of cryptocurrency investments. These records should include dates of transactions, value in fiat currency at the time of the transaction, and the cost basis. This comprehensive record-keeping will facilitate easier calculation of capital gains or losses during tax season.

10.5. How Cryptocurrency Taxes Work Internationally

While we've discussed cryptocurrency tax obligations predominantly in the context of the U.S, it's important to note that these principles differ internationally. Most countries tax cryptocurrencies, but the rules, rates, and regulations vary widely. As an investor operating across borders, understanding cross-country regulations can be crucial.

10.6. Cryptocurrency Gifts and Donations

While gifting or donating cryptocurrency can be a brilliant way of managing tax obligations, several rules will apply. For instance, in the U.S, donors can avoid paying taxes on appreciated stocks or cryptocurrencies. On the other hand, the recipient assumes the donor's cost basis, taking on any associated capital gain.

Moreover, if you're on the receiving end of a cryptocurrency gift, it's not considered a taxable event until you sell the cryptocurrency.

In the end, understanding the tax implications of cryptocurrency investments is critical for any investor. Incorporating this knowledge into your investment strategy may require professional consultation with a tax advisor experienced in cryptocurrency. This will ensure accuracy in reporting, compliance with the tax laws, and optimal management of your tax obligations. Cryptocurrency offers exciting opportunities, and with the correct tax strategy, you can navigate its waters confidently and efficiently.

Chapter 11. Future Prospects: Where do Cryptocurrencies Go from Here?

Cryptocurrencies have established themselves as a prominent part of the modern financial landscape. Their rise to prominence has been characterized by rapid innovation, unpredictability, and large swings in value. These digital assets, powered by Blockchain technology, have far-reaching implications for various sectors, including finance, supply chain management, and even the arts, through non-fungible tokens (NFTs).

11.1. Blockchain as a Game-Changer

Blockchain, the underlying technology of cryptocurrencies, functions as a distributed ledger, preserving the integrity of transactions and reducing the need for intermediaries. Its potential use cases extend well beyond cryptocurrencies. Enterprises across the globe are harnessing the power of this technology to streamline processes, improve transparency, and fortify security measures. The adoption of Blockchain could escalate in the coming years, which would undoubtedly affect the value and practicality of cryptocurrencies.

11.2. Factors Influencing Future Value

The future value of cryptocurrencies largely depends on a number of factors. These include technological advancements, global regulations, market sentiment, and adoption levels. Understanding these will give investors a qualified perspective on the potential future movements of the cryptocurrency market.

Technological advancements - Cryptocurrencies are a technical invention, thus technology undeniably plays a critical role in their future. Next-generation blockchains are being developed to provide solutions to the existing problems with Scalability and Energy consumption.

Regulation - Global regulation could define the trajectory of cryptocurrencies. Regulatory decisions can immensely sway the market, as they determine how, where, and to what extent people can trade cryptocurrencies.

Market Sentiment - Market sentiment remains a major driver of the valuation of cryptocurrencies. Positive news or endorsements can send values soaring, while hacks or negative press can cause sudden drops.

Adoption Levels - Adoption of cryptocurrency for transactions by businesses and consumers would stabilize the price and create a base of regular demand.

11.3. Emerging Economies and Cryptocurrencies

The future of cryptocurrencies also leans heavily towards their potential adoption in emerging economies. With sometimes unstable local currencies and less-developed financial services sectors, these economies could benefit greatly from the decentralization cryptocurrencies offer. Financial inclusion could be improved drastically, allowing more people than ever before to engage in economic activity and wealth creation. This adoption could significantly increase the global demand for cryptocurrencies, elevating their value in the process.

11.4. Institutional Adoption

Another factor impacting the future prospects of cryptocurrencies is their adoption by institutional players. Financial institutions are starting to acknowledge these digital assets. As we go forward, one can anticipate greater acceptance and understanding of cryptocurrencies among traditional finance entities. Inclusion in traditional financial products, like Index Funds and Exchange Traded Funds (ETFs), would lead to significant growth in the overall size of the cryptocurrency market and could offer an additional layer of stability.

11.5. Innovations in Financial Technologies

Technological innovations like Decentralized Finance (DeFi) and Smart Contracts have potential implications for the future of cryptocurrencies. DeFi has the potential to completely overhaul the traditional finance system by rendering a good part of it obsolete, creating a decentralized financial system that operates without intermediaries. Meanwhile, Smart Contracts operate automatically when conditions are met, significantly increasing efficiency and reducing the need for trust.

11.6. The Role of Bitcoin

As the biggest and most recognized cryptocurrency, Bitcoin's journey from here will have significant influence on the overall cryptocurrency market. Having already demonstrated its value as a store of value and "digital gold", the future outlook for Bitcoin will likely be strongly tied to its acceptance as a collateral asset in financial transactions and a trusted mechanism for transfer of value across digital networks.

11.7. Final Thoughts

Looking ahead, it's clear that cryptocurrencies hold significant potential. This potential, however, is paired with considerable volatility and uncertainty. At this stage, we can conclude that cryptocurrencies are here to stay, and will likely only grow in prominence and acceptance in the coming years. Their exact place in our future economy though, is still being written.

Investors must stay informed, grasping onto the latest developments and trends in the sector. Armed with understanding and wisdom, they can make discerning choices in this unpredictable yet exciting arena. Always remember that investing in cryptocurrencies should be approached with caution, with an eye on the potential risks and rewards.